Delicious Drinks

Delicious Drinks

to Sip, Slurp, Gulp & Guzzle

Rose Dunnington

LARK BOOKS
A Division of Sterling Publishing Co., Inc.
New York

Editor:
Veronika Alice Gunter

Creative Director
and Cover Design:
Celia Naranjo

Designer:
Robin Gregory

Stylist:
Skip Wade

Art Assistant:
Bradley Norris

Art Intern:
Ardyce E. Alspach

Photographer:
Steve Mann

Library of Congress Cataloging-in-Publication Data

Dunnington, Rose.
  Delicious drinks to sip, slurp, gulp & guzzle / by Rose
Dunnington.— 1st ed.
      p. cm.
  Includes index.
  ISBN 1-57990-779-2 (hardcover)
  1. Beverages. I. Title.
TX815.D86 2006
641.8'75—dc22

                                    2005030432

10 9 8 7 6 5 4 3 2 1

First Edition

Published by Lark Books, A Division of
Sterling Publishing Co., Inc.
387 Park Avenue South, New York, N.Y. 10016

Text © 2006, Rose Dunnington
Photography © 2006, Lark Books

Distributed in Canada by Sterling Publishing,
c/o Canadian Manda Group, 165 Dufferin Street
Toronto, Ontario, Canada M6K 3H6

Distributed in the United Kingdom by GMC Distribution Services,
Castle Place, 166 High Street, Lewes, East Sussex, England BN7 1XU

Distributed in Australia by Capricorn Link (Australia) Pty Ltd.,
P.O. Box 704, Windsor, NSW 2756 Australia

If you have questions or comments about this book, please contact:
Lark Books
67 Broadway
Asheville, NC 28801
(828) 253-0467

Manufactured in China

ISBN 13: 978-1-57990-779-2
ISBN 10: 1-57990-779-2

For information about custom editions, special sales, and premium and corporate purchases, please
contact Sterling Special Sales Department at 800-805-5489 or specialsales@sterlingpub.com.

This book is dedicated to my sip, slurp, gulp & guzzle crew:

Laura Louise, Philo, Ben, Lilly, Eva, and Johnny.

You're the best siblings a girl could ever have!

Smoothies

Smooth Operator: Pretty in Pink,
Plain Jane, Peachy Keen   16

Breakfast Blend   18

Just the Fruits, Ma'am: The Three P's,
Tropical Delight, Chill Out   20

Drink Your Veggies   22

Berry Bonanza   24

Yam Fan   26

Old School   28

Adventures in Avocado Land:
Not Guac, Pinacado   30

Slush Your Mouth:
Summer in a Glass, Melon Mania,
Cool Daddy-O   32

Milkshake Fake-Out: Bodacious
Bananas, Fruity Tooty, Cloud Nine   34

Ectoplasm   36

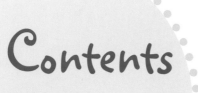

Contents

Dedication   5

Drink Up!   8

Getting Started 10

Coolness

A Little Bit 'o Fizz: Limon Fizz,
Grape Escape, Sparkle Orange   38

Fizzling Apple Slime   40

La La Lassis: Coco-Lala, A Little Nutmeggy,
Marvelous Mango, Cool as a Cucumber   42

Apfelschorle   44

Almond Joy: Apple-icious, Almost Heaven   46

Shirley Temple   48

Sodalicious: Not-So-Plain Vanilla,
Knock-Your-Socks-Off Ginger Ale,
Sassy Root Beer   50

Horchata por mis Amigos:
Horchaloupe, Horchata   52

Forage Teas: Mint, Bee Balm,
Hibiscus, Chamomile, Sassafras,
Rose Hips, Lemon Balm   54

Hot Stuff

Warm and Cozy: Sugar and
Spice, Loco Cocoa, Hot Vanilla   80

The Bee's Knees   82

Mexican Hot Chocolate   84

Sensational Cinnamon Tea   86

Frozen

Blueberry Blast   56

Chocolate Sneezer Shakes   58

Munchy Mix-Ups:
The Kooky Cookie,
Peanut Butter Cup in a Cup   60

Float Away:
Classic Root Beer Float,
Orange Dream, Luscious Lime   62

Black Hole   64

Peanut Butter Lover?:
PB&J Shake, Monkey Shine   66

Crispy Cane   68

Luau Shake: The Shake,
Ooey Gooey Sauce   70

The Big Freeze   72

Batidos: Batido Lindo,
Coconutty Buddy,
Mmmmango   74

Piña Collision   76

Papa Shake   78

Party Drinks

Neon Slurp   88

Guanabana Cabana   90

Double Duty Pink and Fruity:
Hot Magenta, Punch Out   92

Strawberry Sweetheart   94

Knock-Your-Socks-Off
Key Lime Punch   96

Razzle Dazzle   98

Swait Tay   100

First Ades   102

Agua de Tamarindo   104

Which Cider You On?   106

Mull it Over   108

Glossary   110

Metric Conversions   112

Index   112

Drink Up!

Want to drink exactly what you're thirsty for—hot or cold, sweet or zesty, bubbly or creamy — anytime you choose?

I'll show you how easy, quick, and fun it is to make smoothies, floats, teas, sodas, and more.

I've crammed this book with more than 75 fantastic recipes. You'll find familiar favorites, such as hot chocolate, banana smoothies, and milkshakes, as well as tons of drinks you've never heard of. (Ectoplasm, anyone?) I've included neat drinks from all over the world—Batidos, Lassis, and Apfelschorle, to name a few. You'll also find cool ideas to give your creations extra flair when you serve them to friends or family. They'll love these drinks: they taste better than any syrupy-sweet, additive-filled drink boxes or cans you buy off the shelf. (And these drinks are better for you.)

Are you new to the kitchen?
Don't worry about it. I'll tell you everything you need to know about making drinks, from choosing the best fruit for Slush Your Mouth to warming a mug for Loco Cocoa. If you're already a good cook, I'll give you some new ideas. (Ever drunk an avocado? See page 30. Try your hand at almond milk on page 46.)

The Getting Started section shows and tells you the basics to making any drink delicious. Here's where you'll learn how to measure (just how much is a dash?) and how to be a blender wizard. You'll also find cool tricks like how to dice a mango in its peel and how to hull strawberries with a spoon.

How do you find what you're craving?

The recipes are divided into five chapters:

The Smoothies chapter is filled with drinks that are perfect with breakfast, after school, or anytime you need an energy boost between meals. The fresh fruits and healthful ingredients in every gulp will make your body happy, and the intense flavors will put a smile on your lips.

My recipes for Coolness include two dozen iced drinks. Guzzle these to quench your thirst and tingle your taste buds. Try everything from fizzy Grape Escape soda or a cinnamon-flavored Horchata to creamy Coco-Lala.

What's cooler than cool? Ice cold! Flip to the Frozen chapter for frosty, decadent treats. Here you'll find thick, creamy milkshakes, frothy floats, and more. Make your best friend a Piña Collision, or treat yourself to a minty Crispy Cane.

The steamy drinks in Hot Stuff will warm you right up. On a chilly day, there's nothing better than cuddling up with your pet and sipping one of these concoctions from your favorite mug. The Bee's Knees is just one of my sweet and soothing recipes, while Mexican Hot Chocolate spices up a classic.

Make any occasion special with a recipe from my Party Drinks chapter. How about serving piping hot cups of Mull It Over at a holiday get together, or a cool pitcher of Guanabana Cabana punch at a pool party?

Whatever you're in the mood to drink, you'll find it here. Have a blast using this book to satisfy your thirst.

Getting Started

Even if you can't tell a smoothie from a shake or a lassi from sweet tea, soon you'll know more than the average adult about mouth-watering drinks.

Once you've chosen which drink you want to make, read the recipe all the way through so you know exactly what you'll use and how you'll use it. Below the recipe title I tell you how much each recipe makes, such as, "1 to 2 servings." That's the **yield.** I generally give you a range for the yield because I don't know how thirsty you are, or what size glass or cup you are using to serve each drink.

You can double or halve a recipe, depending on how many people you want to serve. If you haven't mastered fractions yet, get an adult to check your math.

After the yield you'll see the recipe's list of ingredients, followed by the instructions. Most of these drinks are blended (see Blending on page 15) or mixed by hand in a punch bowl, pitcher, or serving glass.

Rules, Rules, Rules

Before you start, you'll need to talk with your parents about the rules for using your kitchen. Follow the rules—even if you think they're silly. You'll show your parents that you're trustworthy, which is important.

If you're unsure of any terms, check back in this section, or turn to the glossary on pages 110 to 111. (The glossary is also where you'll find the words you see in bold, **like this.**)

Going Shopping

Do you help with your family's grocery shopping? Well the time has come, my friend, to graduate from just pushing the cart. Most of these drinks are made from **produce,** so the best places to shop for your ingredients are **farmers' markets** or grocery stores. If a fruit you need for a recipe is not **in season** in your area, the frozen food section of a grocery store is the best place to buy it. That's because the fruit was ripe when it was frozen and retains that good flavor.

Tips for Buying Produce

The way something looks isn't the best way to tell how it will taste because speckles, moderate color variations, and funny shapes don't affect flavor. But do use your eyes to spy cuts and **bruises;** imperfect looks are okay, but don't buy damaged fruits.

Some fruits have strong scents that help you gauge **ripeness.** If a fruit smells good when you sniff near its **stem scar,** it's just about **ripe** and worth buying now. If a fruit gives off a very strong pleasant scent, buy it and use it within 24 hours. If a fruit smells musty or rotten, don't buy it. (Duh!)

Avocados and lemons don't have much scent. Use your hands to assess them by gently squeezing the fruit, as Gus is doing in the photo on the left. If it's ripe, it will give slightly. Too soft equals rotten. Rock solid means **unripe.** Unripe is okay if you have a few days to wait for it to ripen. Watermelons require the **thunk test** to determine their ripeness. That means flipping it with your finger as if it were your brother's head. Unlike your brother's head, a watermelon should sound hollow.

Yogurt, Milk, and More

I use plain yogurt in some of these recipes, and I really do mean PLAIN. If you substitute vanilla yogurt, use less honey or sugar or skip the sweetener altogether. Of course, if you like things sweeter than I do, maybe the original amount is just right.

Some of the recipes have milk in their ingredient lists. You can use the kind of milk you prefer, **cow's milk, soymilk,** whatever. In fact, I have recipes for **rice milk** and **almond milk** (pages 52 and 47) that you can make yourself. Whenever you use cow's milk, I recommend you buy **organic,** so you aren't gulping **growth hormones.**

Looking for pear nectar, star anise, vanilla beans, or anything that sounds unusual to you? Nectar is a juice, so you'll find it in the juice aisle. Star anise and vanilla are spices, sold in the spice aisle. If you can't find an ingredient where you shop, look for it at a gourmet shop or health food store. Can't find something? Ask.

Back in the Kitchen

Ready to start making drinks? Tie back your hair (if it's long), remove dangling jewelry, and wash your hands. I recommend wearing an apron if the recipe has ingredients that stain, like blueberries or chocolate, or any time you're wearing your favorite shirt.

Wash, Rinse, Dry

Some produce may look clean, but it can have invisible **bacteria** or **pesticides** on it that need to be washed away. Cool running water usually does the trick, but a drop of dish soap doesn't hurt as long as you rinse well. Use a **colander** for small items like blueberries and pick out any bad pieces, leaves, or stems.

Many people don't think about it, but even fruits that are going to be peeled should be washed first. This is because the knife can pick up bacteria from the outside and transfer it to the part you're going to eat. Okay, so you don't have to wash bananas before you peel them.

Dry the produce after you wash it. If it needs to be cut, you don't want it to be wet and slippery. If you're just going to throw it in the blender, you don't want extra water to **dilute** the flavor.

Tools

Most of my recipes use just a couple of basic kitchen tools: **knife, measuring cups, blender,** etc. (Read about blenders on page 15.) A few of the recipes call for specialized tools, and the recipe directions will say so. You can find descriptions of basic and special kitchen tools in the glossary.

Using Knives

A kitchen knife is kind of like a skateboard —with practice, you can do really cool stuff, but if you aren't careful you'll get hurt. If you're using a knife, you'll need a **cutting board**—and your full attention. Pause all conversations until you finish with the knife.

There are lots of kinds of knives, but there's only one safe way to use a knife. Make a claw out of the hand that you don't write with, tucking the thumb behind the finger-tips. (It looks a bit like the letter E in sign language.) Use that claw to hold down the food you're chopping. The thumb can guide the food forward just as long as it stays behind the fingers. Never raise the blade (the cutting edge) of the knife higher than the knuckles of your guiding hand.

Speaking of knives, wash a knife as soon as you're finished using it. NEVER put a knife in a sink full of soapy water. It might cut the next person (and that could be you!) who reaches into the sink. It's also bad for the knife.

Since the fruits you cut up for these recipes are going to be **liquefied,** it doesn't matter what the chunks look like. Just cut them into **cubes** of about 1-inch.

Really soft foods, such as fresh bananas or baked sweet potatoes, can just be tossed in the blender whole.

A few fruits require some special attention: To use a melon, first cut the melon in half. Get an adult to do this step if your melon's extra big, or your knife gets stuck. Use a spoon to scrape out the seeds. Cut the halves into **wedges**. (I usually make four wedges from each half.) Carefully cut the flesh from the **rind.** See top left photo. Have an adult help as needed. Now chop the melon flesh.

To chop up a pineapple, first cut the top and bottom off, so the pineapple sits flat on the cutting board. Carefully cut the rind off in strips. See the cut away rind in the top right photo. If you miss some of the **spines,** use the pointy end of a **vegetable peeler** to scoop them out. Next, cut the fruit into quarters **lengthwise**. Cut the hard, whitish **core** away. See bottom left photo. Chop the rest into chunks. Too much work? Well, for a little extra money you can buy fresh pineapple already peeled and cored—just cut it into chunks.

A large, flat **pit** runs through the center of a mango, so you must cut to either side of the pit (shown in the lower left corner of the photo below). Then use a table knife to cut a grid pattern in the mango flesh, and turn the mango inside out so it looks like a porcupine. Knock the mango chunks out to eat or use them.

Vanilla beans are often used whole, but some recipes ask you to separate the **seeds** from the **pod**. Slice the vanilla bean in half lengthwise. Gently scrape the seeds out with a spoon. See top photo. The seeds are so tiny they look like black goop. Save the pod to use.

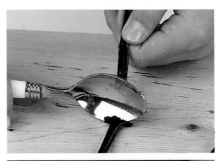

Strawberries need to be **hulled.** Use the tip of a spoon to scoop the stem and leaves from a strawberry. See middle photo on this page. Discard the stem and leaves. Now the strawberry is ready to be used or eaten.

Ginger root needs to be skinned before use. Use the edge of a spoon to scrape the thin skin from the root. See bottom photo. Discard the skin.

Zest is the colored part of the peel of **citrus fruit.** You peel it off with a vegetable peeler or **bar zester,** or use the smallest holes of a **grater.** See pages 78 and 82.

Freezing Fruits

Some of these recipes use frozen fruits to make icy, slushy concoctions. You can buy them frozen or freeze your own. For bananas and melons, though, you'll definitely have to do your own freezing. Follow the directions on page 13 to chop melons. Then put the chunks into resealable plastic freezer bags, and the next day you'll have frozen chunks. Use seedless watermelon or pick the seeds out before you freeze the chunks. Peel bananas and place them whole into freezer bags. To freeze other fruits, do all of the prep work first: wash, dry, peel, seed, chop— whatever is needed. Trust me, it's almost impossible to get the pit out of a frozen peach.

Measuring

You don't have to measure most ingredients in the recipes in this book exactly. When you do measure, you'll generally use **measuring spoons** and **liquid measuring cups,** or buy ingredients in packages of the size indicated in the recipe. Here are some helpful measurement conversions:

2 pinches = 1 dash

2 dashes = 1/8 teaspoon

3 teaspoons = 1 tablespoon

4 tablespoons = 1/4 cup

2 cups = 1 pint

4 cups = 1 quart

1 quart = about 1 liter

Measuring chunks of fruit is not an exact science. I let the tops of some of the chunks rise above the top of the measuring cup. I figure I'd rather have a little bit too much than not enough.

Frozen Solid?

When I freeze fresh fruit, its juice tends to leak out in the bag and form a solid block. So I take the whole bag outside and drop it on a hard surface to break up the chunks. I haven't had an exploding bag disaster yet, but I still do this outside just in case.

Mixing

How you put your ingredients together is an important part of recipe instructions. For instance, your smoothie won't be smooth and slurpable if you just throw the recommended fruit chunks in a cup.

Here are the mixing terms you'll see in the recipes: **Combine** means to mix the ingredients together. **Stir** means to use a spoon or other utensil to mix the ingredients. Sometimes **blend** means the same thing as combine, but in this book, it means that you should use a blender.

Blending

I like to use an **immersion blender** whenever possible. Why? Fewer dishes to wash, of course! Just grab a large cup, big enough to fit all the recipe's ingredients plus the immersion blender, with some room left over for sloshing.

It feels natural to push the immersion blender down on the food, but that's not the way it was designed to work. Instead, hold it so that the **bulb** (the wider part with the **blade**) is **submerged,** but not touching the bottom of the cup. As it blends, the immersion blender will pull chunks up to the blade automatically.

If your recipe doesn't have much liquid to start with (like Ectoplasm on page 36), start with all of the liquid and a few chunks of fruit, and gradually add more chunks as the concoction liquefies.

A regular **standing blender,** like the one you see on this page, works best for recipes that include ice cubes. Standing blenders work just as well as immersion blenders for everything else, too. So use whatever type of blender your family already owns.

Make sure your hands are dry before you plug or unplug any blender, and always unplug it before you change the attachments or clean it. Don't put the base in water when you're cleaning it. You could ruin the motor, and if it's plugged in you could be shocked. Just wipe it with a wrung-out soapy cloth or sponge.

Stovetop Cooking

A few of these recipes require a bit of cooking on the stove. Luckily, this will be easy for you to do safely. Just follow my suggestions and ask for an adult's assistance anytime you have questions or need help.

Choose a pot that's bigger than what you're putting in it so you have room to stir and avoid boiling-over disasters. Aim pot handles towards the middle of the stove so you don't accidentally knock them over.

Use a ladle to transfer hot liquids to serving cups. It's really hard to pour straight from the pot.

If you heat any kind of milk on the stovetop, you really do have to stand there and stir the whole time. Otherwise, the bottom will burn and a skin will develop on the top. Actually, I love this part of cooking—it's relaxing to just stand and stir and think about things. Don't **boil** milk or the texture will change from creamy to grainy.

Serving

Add an extra-special touch to serving your fabulous creations: If you're making a hot drink, fill mugs with hot water so they can warm up as you cook. If it's a frosty treat, stick your tumblers in the freezer while you work. (It's okay to put empty glasses in the freezer, but use plastic cups if you want to store a drink in the freezer. Liquids expand as they freeze and might crack glass.)

Ready to drink up? Turn the page.

smoothies

Smoothies are a sweet pick-me-up. The fruit gives you an instant burst of energy any time of day.

Smooth Operator

I especially love smoothies for breakfast. In fact, I once drank Pretty in Pink every morning for six months! At the time, it was the only smoothie I knew how to make.

Plain Jane Banana Smoothie
1 serving

ingredients

1 banana, peeled
1 cup plain yogurt
2 tablespoons honey

Combine the ingredients and blend until smooth.

Pretty in Pink
1 to 2 servings

ingredients

1 banana, peeled
1 cup plain yogurt
1 cup frozen strawberries
½ cup pineapple juice
1 tablespoon honey

Combine the ingredients and blend until smooth and creamy.

Peachy Keen
1 to 2 servings

ingredients

1 banana, peeled
1 cup plain yogurt
1 cup frozen sliced peaches
½ cup apricot nectar
1 tablespoon honey
⅛ teaspoon nutmeg

Blend the ingredients together until this drink is creamy, smooth, and uniform in color.

Breakfast Blend

The other smoothies in this book are great as part of your breakfast, but this one is a meal all by itself. Complex carbohydrates, like those in rolled oats, are good for you, especially early in the day. It takes your body a while to break carbs down into usable fuel, so Breakfast Blend can keep you full until lunchtime.

1 or 2 servings

ingredients

1 banana, peeled
2 tablespoons peanut butter
2 tablespoons rolled oats
  (old fashioned or quick)
½ cup orange juice
4 frozen strawberries

Combine the ingredients and blend until smooth. This smoothie takes some extra blending time because of the rolled oats. But it's quicker than cooking a plate of eggs and way yummier than bran flakes.

smoothies

Just the Fruits, Ma'am

These 100-percent fruit smoothies are 100-percent delicious. Frozen ingredients make these drinks frosty enough to give you the shivers.

The Three P's
1 to 2 servings

ingredients

1 cup frozen sliced peaches
1 cup peeled and chopped papaya
¾ cup pomegranate juice

Combine the ingredients and blend until smooth and uniform in color. By the way, what would you call the color of this drink?

Tropical Delight
1 to 2 servings

ingredients

1 frozen banana, broken into chunks
1 cup peeled, chopped papaya
¾ cup pineapple juice

Combine and blend until smooth. Try slurping this creamy drink through a wide straw.

Chill Out
1 to 2 servings

ingredients

1 banana, peeled
1 cup frozen cantaloupe chunks
¾ cup apricot nectar

Blend the ingredients together until creamy.

Drink Your Veggies

You know how Popeye gets super-charged when he eats spinach? That's how you'll feel when you sip this tangy veggie smoothie. It's way more fun and delicious than boiled spinach.

1 to 2 servings

ingredients

1 medium-sized tomato, cut into chunks
   (about 1 ½ cups)
half of a cucumber, peeled, seeded, and cut into chunks
   (about 1 cup)
½ cup bell pepper chunks
   (Red, green, or yellow—I used red.)
1 ½ teaspoons fresh lemon juice
½ teaspoon sugar
⅛ teaspoon celery salt
3 or 4 ice cubes

Blend until all of the ingredients are thoroughly combined. Just for fun, use a long cucumber stick as a one-of-a-kind stirrer.

Seeding a Cucumber
Seeding doesn't mean planting; it means removing the seeds. To prepare the cucumber, peel it and cut it in half. Then use the spoon to remove the cucumber seeds. Just slide the spoon into the cut side of one half, pushing away from you. Then cut the cucumber halves into chunks.

Berry Bonanza

This smoothie is sweet, tangy, and filling—perfect for an after-school snack. Berries are super-foods, packed with nutrients. It just so happens that fruits and vegetables that are deeply colored (dark purple, red, green, etc.) are extra good for you. Plus, they're usually extra delicious.

1 to 2 servings

ingredients

1 cup blueberries
1 cup frozen strawberries
1 banana, peeled
½ cup mixed berry juice

Blend everything together until it's uniformly purple. Drink up!

Check your teeth for stray blueberry peels before you flash that grin.

Yam Fan

This smoothie is as yummy as it is unusual. The flavor is similar to that of the candied yams you eat at Thanksgiving, but the o. j. gives it a taste of the tropics. Try it!

1 to 2 servings

ingredients

1 yam or sweet potato, baked
   and peeled (about ½ cup)
½ cup plain yogurt
¾ cup orange juice
⅓ cup caramel sauce
   (See page 70 for a recipe.)

Combine the ingredients.
Blend until smooth.

Fruit Swizzler

Turn up the snack factor of your drinks by adding a fruit kabob stirring stick. Just push bite-sized pieces of fruit onto a wooden skewer. Make one for each serving and have fun stirring and munching.

Yams and sweet potatoes are the roots of different plants, but they're very similar, so you can use either one for this recipe.

Old School

My mother-in-law, Stephanie, gave me the idea for this smoothie. Steph does volunteer work at a daycare, so she's totally hip to what little kids like. I call it Old School because it will take you back to your kindergarten days when the three major food groups were apple juice, peanut butter, and bananas.

1 to 2 servings

ingredients

1 frozen banana, broken into chunks
¾ cup apple juice
2 tablespoons creamy peanut butter
a dash of cinnamon

Combine the ingredients and blend until smooth.

Adventures in Avocado Land

Avocados are used so often with salty and spicy dishes that I sometimes forget that they're fruits. Even better, they're extra-creamy, delicious fruits. I thought maybe avocados could work like bananas in smoothies, so I did some experiments. Here are the recipes. I hope you like them as much as I do.

Not Guac
2 to 3 servings

ingredients

1 avocado
2 tablespoons honey
2 cups milk (I think rice milk is yummiest.)

Blend the avocado flesh and the other ingredients together until smooth. Give it a taste. Isn't that crazy-good?

Scooping Out an Avocado
To prepare the avocado, use a cutting board and a knife and cut it in half. Then remove the pit and use a spoon to scoop out the pulp.

Pinacado
2 to 3 servings

ingredients

1 avocado
1 ½ cups pineapple juice

Blend the avocado flesh and the pineapple juice together until smooth. Drink up!

Slush Your Mouth

There's nothing like a sweet, ripe melon in the summertime. These three recipes up the chill factor by using frozen melons. The taste is just as fantastic, plus they're cold, cold, cold.

Melon Mania
1 serving

ingredients

1 cup frozen cantaloupe chunks
1 cup watermelon chunks (not frozen)

Blend the ingredients until they achieve a thick, smooth consistency. Enjoy.

Summer in a Glass
1 serving

ingredients

1 ½ cups frozen watermelon chunks
¼ cup peach nectar

Combine the ingredients and blend until smooth.

Cool Daddy-O
1 serving

ingredients

1 cup frozen cantaloupe chunks
piece of peeled fresh ginger the size of your knuckle (about 1/2 teaspoon)
½ cup pear nectar
squirt of honey
dash of salt

Blend all the ingredients together until perfectly slushy.

My granddaddies liked to sprinkle a little salt on their cantaloupe for a salty-sweet flavor sensation. Cool Daddy-O borrows that idea and adds ginger for zing.

Milkshake Fake-Out

These three drinks are yummy and healthful enough to enjoy any time of day. Imagine telling your friends, "Oh, you had cereal again? I had a milkshake." You don't have to mention that it was a fake-out.

Bodacious Bananas
1 serving

ingredients

1 frozen banana, broken into chunks
1/2 cup milk (I like soy milk.)
1 tablespoon chocolate syrup

Combine the ingredients and blend until smooth.

Cloud Nine
1 to 2 servings

ingredients

1 frozen banana, broken into chunks
1/2 cup frozen strawberries
3/4 cup unsweetened coconut milk

Blend all the ingredients together until—you guessed it—smooth.

Fruity Tooty
1 to 2 servings

ingredients

1 frozen banana, broken into chunks
1 cup pineapple chunks
3/4 cup pear nectar

Blend until smooth.

Ectoplasm

Have you seen the movie Ghostbusters? Maybe you've only seen the cartoon, but pshaw to that. The movie is a classic, and it's a lot like this drink—shivery, giggly, and sour-sweet. This is my husband Steve's favorite drink in this book.

2 to 3 servings

ingredients

2 cups frozen honeydew chunks
¾ cup guanabana juice (What's guanabana? See page 90.)
1 kiwi, peeled and chopped

Blend the frozen honeydew with the guanabana juice until smooth and slushy. Then add the kiwi and blend a little more. Voilá! Ectoplasm.

I recommend a wide straw for drinking this. Don't have one? You can either wait for the Ectoplasm to melt some, or add more guanabana juice and re-blend until it's a thinner consistency.

coolness

Ultimate Coolness!
That's what this chapter's
all about.

A Little Bit o' Fizz

Maybe I'm a complete whacko, but I've never liked the flavor of store-bought sodas, not even when I was a kid. But I love these! They're a cross between juice and soda. These bubbly, fruity, chilly drinks are perfectly refreshing on their own, but they also go great with a meal.

Limon Fizz
1 serving

ingredients

4 teaspoons limeade concentrate
1 ½ cups sparkling water
(seltzer or club soda)

Stir the juice concentrate into the sparkling water. Add ice and serve.

Sparkle Orange
1 serving

ingredients

2 tablespoons orange juice concentrate
1 ½ cups sparkling water (seltzer or club soda)

Stir the juice concentrate into the sparkling water. Add ice and—you guessed it—serve.

Grape Escape
1 serving

ingredients

2 tablespoons grape juice concentrate
(Make sure you get 100% juice, or it will have a nasty fake-grape flavor.)
1 ½ cups sparkling water (seltzer or club soda)

Stir the juice concentrate into the sparkling water. Add ice and serve. (I served it over frozen grapes instead.)

coolness

Fizzling Apple Slime

This is a weird one—but weird in a good way. The textures of the dissolving apple gelatin and the fizzy ginger ale combine for a unique drinking experience. Use a straw to suck it up, and then swish it around in your mouth. Plan ahead: The apple gelatin has to chill in the refrigerator for several hours before you make this drink.

4 servings

ingredients

1 ¼ cups apple juice

1 tablespoon unflavored gelatin (find it in the grocery's gelatin and pudding aisle)

1 inch strip of lemon zest

1 liter ginger ale

For each serving, loosely fill a glass halfway with apple gelatin flakes. (See below). Top it off with ginger ale.

Making the Apple Gelatin Flakes

Sprinkle the unflavored gelatin over ¼ cup of apple juice. Let it set while you do the next step.
In a saucepot over a medium burner, heat the remaining cup of apple juice with the lemon zest until it steams but doesn't bubble. Turn off the stove.
Add the gelatin mixture to the warm apple juice and stir to dissolve. Pour this mixture into a storage container or baking dish. Leave it in the refrigerator, covered, until it solidifies (at least 4 hours).
Scrape a fork through the apple gelatin to break it up in to small flakes.

La La Lassis

A lassi is a yogurt drink from India. (Pronounce it "Lah-see.")
It goes well with spicy foods because it cools your mouth.
Traditional lassis are salty and include mild spices such as cumin.
I make mine sweet. Serve them with or without ice—your choice.

Coco-Lala
1 serving

ingredients

¾ cup plain yogurt
¼ cup sweetened coconut cream
2 ice cubes

Since you are using ice cubes, you may want to use a standard blender rather than an immersion blender. Blend until creamy.

A Little Nutmeggy
1 serving

ingredients

1 cup plain yogurt
1 ½ teaspoons sugar
2 ice cubes
pinch of nutmeg

Just blend until smooth. Enjoy.

Marvelous Mango
1 or 2 servings

ingredients

1 mango, pitted, peeled, and chopped
   (See page 13.)
¾ cup plain yogurt
1 to 2 teaspoons sugar (depends on
   how sweet the mango is)
2 ice cubes

Blend until smooth. The mango turns this drink a gorgeous color.

Cool as a Cucumber
1 serving

ingredients

½ cup peeled and seeded cucumber
   chunks (See page 22.)
½ cup plain yogurt
½ teaspoon fresh mint leaves
1 teaspoon sugar

Blend all the ingredients together until smooth.

Apfelschorle

My German friend Franziska guzzles this drink to cool down after energetic tennis games. "Apfelschorle" means "sparkling apple" in German. "Sparkling apple juice" is "apfelsaftschorle," but German kids shorten it.

as many servings as you want

ingredients

apple juice
sparkling water (club soda or seltzer)
lemon wedges (optional)

No need to measure! Just pour equal parts of apple juice and sparkling water over ice. For extra zing, squeeze a little fresh lemon juice into each glass.

Almond Joy

Betcha didn't know you could get milk from almonds! The flavor is clean and slightly sweet. To follow these recipes, first you make the Liquid Nuts. Drink it straight or follow the recipes to combine it with other ingredients.

Apple-icious
1 to 2 servings

ingredients

1 recipe Liquid Nuts (See this page.)
1 cup apple juice
dash of ground cinnamon

Combine all of the ingredients. Serve chilled. Stir if the ingredients separate before you finish drinking.

Making Liquid Nuts

Grind 1 cup of almonds in a food processor or blender until they are very fine. Add 1½ cups of water and let the mixture soak for a couple of minutes. In the meantime, drape a clean kitchen towel inside a mixing bowl. Pour the soaked almond mixture into the cloth. Gather the excess cloth up and twist to make a bundle. Now squeeze over the bowl! Squeeze all the milk you can into the bowl. Discard the almond paste, unless you want to experiment using it in a food recipe.

Almost Heaven
1 to 2 servings

ingredients

1 recipe Liquid Nuts (See this page.)
2 cups frozen sliced peaches
1 tablespoon honey
pinch of nutmeg

Blend the ingredients until they're creamy like a milkshake.

Liquid Nuts keeps for up to a week in a sealed container in the refrigerator. The ingredients separate, but a simple stir takes care of that.

Shirley Temple

When I told my friends I was writing a kids' drink book they all said the same thing: "You have to do Shirley Temples!" My friends weren't literally thinking of the 1930s child movie star, the eponym of this classic for-kids cocktail. They were remembering how fancy they used to feel sipping this drink in restaurants.

as many servings as you like

ingredients

ice

ginger ale

grenadine (sold in the beverage aisle
   of the grocery store)

maraschino cherries

Fill a glass with ice and ginger ale. Add a splash of grenadine (about 1 tablespoon—enough to give a rosy color). Garnish with a maraschino cherry or two. Act sophisticated while you sip this drink. (No playing with the cherry.)

Sodalicious

These sodas are really neat: you make a batch of syrup and then add a little bit to sparkling water when you're thirsty. Store these syrups in a sealed container in the refrigerator for up to two weeks.

Sassy Root Beer

12 or more servings

ingredients

1 handful (¼ to ¾ cup) sassafras root
   (See page 55.)
2 cups sugar
1 cup water
1 cup sparkling water (seltzer or club soda)

Follow the instructions for Knock-Your-Socks-Off Ginger Ale, except substitute sassafras for ginger. To make one soda, stir 1 tablespoon of syrup into ¾ cup of sparkling water. Serve over ice.

Not-So-Plain Vanilla

12 or more servings

ingredients

1 vanilla bean pod (See page 14.)
2 cups sugar
1 cup water
sparkling water (seltzer or club soda)

Stir the sugar and water together in a medium-sized cooking pot. Add the vanilla bean pod and bring to a boil on a stovetop over medium-high heat. Stir occasionally. Reduce the heat to medium and boil 1 to 2 minutes. To make one soda, stir 1 tablespoon of syrup into ¾ cup of sparkling water. Serve over ice.

Knock-Your-Socks-Off Ginger Ale

12 or more servings

ingredients

½ cup peeled and sliced fresh ginger root
   (See page 14.)
1 cup water
2 cups sugar
1 cup sparkling water (seltzer or club soda)

Stir the sugar and water together in a medium-sized cooking pot. Add the ginger, and bring to a boil on a stovetop over medium-high heat. Stir occasionally. Reduce the heat to medium and boil 5 to 7 minutes. To make one soda, stir 1 tablespoon of syrup into ¾ cup of sparkling water. Serve over ice.

Horchata por mis Amigos

This sweet cinnamon-flavored drink is popular in Mexico. You pronounce it, "or-CHA-tah." It's made from rice, but it's way better than the rice milk you buy at the store. (And I think that kind is pretty good). If you like, add ¼ teaspoon of vanilla extract, or a squeeze of fresh lime juice. Don't like nuts? Leave out the almonds and increase the rice to 1 cup.

Horchaloupe
1 to 2 servings

ingredients

¾ cup Horchata
(See recipe on this page.)
1 cup frozen cantaloupe chunks

Combine the ingredients and blend until smooth. Enjoy.

Horchata stays fresh in a sealed container in the refrigerator for up to a week. Stir it well before you drink it.

Horchata
3 to 4 servings

ingredients

¾ cup uncooked rice
½ cup raw almonds
1 cinnamon stick
4 cups water,
plus some extra
½ cup sugar

Rinse the rice, and then combine it with the almonds, cinnamon stick, and 4 cups of water in a medium-sized storage container or mixing bowl. Cover and leave in the refrigerator overnight.

The next day purée the ingredients in a blender until the rice and almonds are in tiny pieces, like sand. Remove what's left of the cinnamon stick.

Drape a kitchen towel inside a mixing bowl. Pour the rice mixture into the cloth. Gather the excess cloth up and twist to make a bundle. Now squeeze! See the photo on page 47 for the same technique. Discard the paste that remains in the cloth.

Add enough water to the rice milk to total 4 cups of liquid. Stir in the sugar and serve. (I like Horchata best chilled, but it's also yummy served warm.)

Forage Teas

To get the ingredients for these yummy teas go to the original grocery store: the great outdoors. If you're not familiar with what these plants look like, use a plant identification book or look them up on the Internet. While you're at it, see if you can find some I haven't mentioned. Do your foraging the right way: for every plant you take, make sure there are two left in the wild.

2 to 4 servings

ingredients

1 quart water, boiling
your choice of herb (See this page.)
honey, to taste

To make any Forage Tea, follow these instructions:

Place a couple of handfuls of well-washed plant material in a medium to large bowl or pitcher. Pour about 1 quart of boiling water into the bowl.

Allow the tea to **steep** for 5 to 7 minutes. (Taste to decide when the flavor is strong enough for you. You could steep for longer or shorter than I recommend.)

Sweeten with honey. (Taste to decide how much honey to use.) To serve, strain the tea into tumblers or cups filled with ice. Don't use glasses—the sudden temperature change might cause them to crack.

Mint
Use the leaves and flowers.

Bee Balm
Use the leaves and flowers of this wild mint.

Hibiscus
Use the red flowers.

Chamomile
Use the little daisy-like flowers.

Sassafras
Dig up small seedlings (found around a fully grown tree) and use the roots.

Rose Hips
These are the fruits of roses. Choose ripe, reddish-orange ones.

Lemon Balm
Use the leaves of this herb.

frozen

The frozen drinks in this chapter are
decadent and frosty.

Blueberry Blast

Got the summertime blues? Blueberry Blast
is a sure cure for those heat-wave doldrums.
It's creamy. It's freezy. It's purple.
It's just right for slurping on a
hot, muggy afternoon.

1 to 2 servings

ingredients

2 cups vanilla ice cream
1 cup washed blueberries
¼ cup milk

Blend all the ingredients together
until you have a delicious purple
concoction. This drink is thick,
so you might need a straw
and a spoon.

Chocolate Sneezer Shakes

My mom, my sister Laura Louise, and I are the only people I've met who sneeze when we eat chocolate. That doesn't stop us! (Actually, I think sneezing's kind of fun.) These two shakes combine luscious chocolate with yummy fruits. If you haven't had this combination before, you're in for a treat.

Choco-Berry
1 to 2 servings

ingredients

2 cups chocolate ice cream
1/2 to 3/4 cup milk
1 cup frozen raspberries

Blend until smooth.

Choco-Nana
1 to 2 servings

ingredients

2 cups chocolate ice cream
1 banana, peeled
1/4 cup milk

Blend the ingredients together until smooth. Take a sip. Can you believe how good this tastes?

Munchy Mix-Ups

These two shakes are over-the-top. If you earned an A on a test, you should totally reward yourself with one of these outrageous treats.

Peanut Butter Cup in a Cup
1 to 2 servings

ingredients

2½ cups chocolate ice cream
2 tablespoons creamy peanut butter
⅓ cup peanut butter cup candies
¼ cup milk

Combine and blend just until the mixture is still a little chunky. If you have leftover candies, break them into pieces and sprinkle them on top of each serving of shake.

The Kooky Cookie
1 to 2 servings

ingredients

2½ cups vanilla ice cream
⅔ cup broken chocolate sandwich cookies
¼ cup milk

Blend the ingredients together just until the mixture is still a little chunky. Break a few extra cookies into small pieces and use them to garnish each drink.

My brother Johnny is a candy fanatic. These are his favorite shakes.

Float Away

In the 1950s soda fountains were hangout places where you'd meet your friends for frothy ice cream and soda concoctions called floats. The people who worked there were called soda jerks. I think anyone who makes me one of these frosty treats is super sweet.

as many servings as you like

ingredients

ice cream or sherbet (See options below.)
soda (See options below.)

To make the float of your choice, follow these instructions:

Put two scoops of ice cream or sherbet in a glass and top it off with the soda. Drink with a straw.

Classic Root Beer Float

Use vanilla ice cream and root beer.

Orange Dream

Use orange sherbet and vanilla soda.

Luscious Lime

Use lime sherbet and ginger ale.

Try my homemade soda recipes on page 51 in these floats.

Black Hole

My father is one of those weird individuals who just doesn't care for sweets. Seriously—he'd rather eat bread than cake. The only desserts that are sure to tempt him are chocolate-cherry combos like this float. I'm crazy about this drink too. In fact, this might be my favorite float, although it's hard to choose.

as many servings as you like

ingredients

chocolate ice cream

black cherry soda
  (The all-natural kind has the most flavor.)

whipped cream
  (See optional recipe on this page.)

cherry garnish (optional)

For each serving, put two scoops of ice cream in a glass and top it off with soda. If you want, add whipped cream and a cherry on top.

Whipped Cream

Combine ½ pint heavy whipping cream with 1 tablespoon sugar and ½ teaspoon vanilla extract in a medium-sized mixing bowl. Whip until stiff. Use a large spoon to put a dollop on top of each float. Don't forget to lick the spoon when you're done. This makes enough to top 6 floats.

Peanut Butter Lover?

If so, these are your shakes. Take your pick of peanut butter paired with chocolate or fruit, or make them both. But you'd better plan to share half of each with a friend, because these drinks will fill you up fast.

PB&J Shake
1 to 2 servings

ingredients

2 cups vanilla ice cream
3 tablespoons creamy peanut butter
¼ cup fruity pancake syrup (I like blueberry.)

Combine the ingredients and blend until they're smooth and uniform in color.

Monkey Shine
1 to 2 servings

ingredients

1 cup vanilla ice cream
half of a banana, peeled
1½ teaspoons cocoa powder
1 tablespoon peanut butter
¼ cup milk

Blend until it's all creamy.

Crispy Cane

My friend Andrew named this tongue-numbing shake for its tiny candy-cane flavored ingredients. I'm not kidding about the tongue numbing part: This super-minty recipe is more intensely refreshing than a whole pack of gum.

1 to 2 servings

ingredients

¼ cup hard peppermint candies, crushed (See instructions on right.)
2 cups vanilla ice cream
⅛ teaspoon peppermint extract
¼ cup milk

Blend the ingredients until the texture is smooth. You should see small flakes of candy in the finished drink, but if you see chunks larger than a raisin, blend some more.

Crushing Candies

This is fun, but be careful. Put the unwrapped peppermint candies in a sandwich bag. If it's the sealable kind, don't seal it. Put the bag on a cutting board. Whack the bag of candy with the flat side of a meat tenderizer or the bottom of a small frying pan to break the candy into small pieces. You'll need to whack it several times.
Okay, so we forgot to use the bag. We're still finding candy pieces all over the kitchen!

Like chocolate with your mint?
Replace the vanilla ice cream with chocolate ice cream.

Luau Shake

Here's a creamy beverage that's sweetened with gooey caramel sauce. Pretend you're in Hawaii while you drink it. Unless, of course, you really are in Hawaii, in which case, well, lucky you!

The Shake
2 to 3 servings

ingredients

2 cups vanilla ice cream
2 cups frozen pineapple chunks
1/3 cup Ooey Gooey Sauce (A light coating of non-stick cooking spray will keep the sauce from sticking to your measuring cup. See recipe on this page.)

Blend the ingredients together until smooth. To make your shake look like the one in the photo, drizzle extra sauce in the glass before you pour in the shake.

Ooey Gooey Sauce
Makes 1 1/2 cups of sauce

ingredients

14 ounce package of soft caramel candies, unwrapped
2/3 cup milk

Combine both ingredients in a medium-sized cooking pot and heat on a stovetop over medium-high heat. Stir occasionally, until the candies have melted into the milk.

Ooey Gooey Sauce will keep for up to a week in a sealed container in the refrigerator. It's also yummy as an ice cream topping or a dip for apple slices.

The Big Freeze

My friend Rebekah told me about this recipe, which was her favorite after-school treat. If you like oranges and ice cream this could become your favorite drink.

1 to 2 servings

ingredients

2 cups vanilla ice cream

2 tablespoons frozen orange
    juice concentrate

¼ cup orange juice

Combine the ingredients
and blend until creamy
and smooth.

Butterfly Garnish

This garnish looks cool, and it's easy to make. You'll
need a toothpick, a thin slice of orange, and a
maraschino cherry for each butterfly. Twist the orange
to make two wings. Stick the toothpick through
the cherry and the overlapping orange peel.

73

Batidos

These are milkshakes made from fresh fruit and sweetened condensed milk. Batidos (bah-TEE-dose) were invented in Latin America. In cities like Havana and Miami, venders push batido carts around and you can buy one of these sweet, creamy drinks to enjoy on the beach. They are super-sweet, so don't drink too much or you'll suffer from batido-belly.

Batido Lindo

2 to 3 servings

ingredients

1 cup sweetened condensed milk
juice of one lime
1½ cups hulled strawberries
12 ice cubes

Blend until—guess what?—smooth and creamy. Which Batido is your favorite?

Mmmmango

2 to 3 servings

ingredients

1 cup sweetened condensed milk
2 mangos, peeled and pitted
12 ice cubes

Combine the ingredients and blend them until you have a smooth, creamy drink that's uniform in color.

Coconutty Buddy

2 to 3 servings

ingredients

1 cup sweetened condensed milk
1 cup unsweetened coconut milk
⅛ teaspoon ground cinnamon
12 ice cubes

Blend the ingredients together until smooth and creamy.

I recommend using a standing blender with the lid on tight for these, so the ice cubes don't go flying across the kitchen.

Piña Collision

The ingredients are all fruit, but don't let that fool you! Sweetened coconut cream is seriously sweet, making this shake a dessert or special treat. If you have a hammock, I recommend lounging in it while you slurp your Piña Collision.

2 to 3 servings

ingredients

1 cup pineapple juice

1 cup sweetened coconut cream (sold in cans in the cocktail mixers section of the grocery store)

2 cups frozen pineapple chunks

Combine the ingredients and blend until smooth. Wanna serve the drink in coconut cups? Read how below.

Coconut Cups

Make two neat serving cups out of a real coconut! All you need is a coconut, a bowl, and a cleaver. If the coconut and/or cleaver feel too big for you to be in total control, or you are at all uncomfortable doing this, get an adult to do it for you.

Here's what you'll do: First, have a bowl ready nearby to catch the coconut juice. Picture an imaginary line around the middle of the coconut. Tap this line with the dull edge of a cleaver. Don't whack it! Just keep tapping until the coconut splits in half (it could take as many as twenty taps). Move the coconut over the bowl and let the juice drain into the bowl. (You can drink the juice later.) Your cup is ready to be filled.

Warning: The coconut cups won't stand up by themselves. Hold your cup in one hand while you drink your Piña Collision. When you're done with your drink, you can eat the white coconut meat from the coconut halves. Get an adult to cut it away from the brown shell. (I'm not suggesting that you get an adult to do it because I don't think you can handle it—I'm saying it because this step is a pain in the neck!)

Papa Shake

This shake is named after the writer Ernest Hemingway, nicknamed Papa. During the later part of his life, Hemingway lived in Key West, Florida, and loved drinks made with key lime juice. Unless you live in Florida, you probably can't buy the special little key limes. That's okay. This recipe cheats a little with limeade concentrate.

1 to 2 servings

ingredients

2 cups vanilla ice cream
2 tablespoons frozen limeade concentrate
¼ cup milk
1 tablespoon finely grated lime zest

Combine the ingredients and blend until creamy.

Curly Q's

Want to recreate the cool garnish you see in the photograph of Papa Shake? Just grab a bar zester and a lime. Pull the small holes of a bar zester across the fruit to get little strips of zest. Wrap the strips around your little finger to curl them. Put some strips on the top of each drink after you've poured it into the serving glasses.

hot stuff

These drinks are perfect to sip while you cuddle up with a good book.

Warm and Cozy

Loco Cocoa is an extra-rich version of classic hot chocolate. Hot Vanilla is speckled like your favorite vanilla ice cream, and just as delicious. Sugar and Spice is ultra relaxing thanks to the cloves and star anise, which tastes like licorice.

Sugar and Spice

3 to 4 servings

ingredients

4 cups milk
⅓ cup brown sugar
½ teaspoon vanilla extract
4 star anise
1 teaspoon whole cloves
1 cinnamon stick

Combine all of the ingredients in a medium-sized cooking pot. Heat on a stovetop over a medium-low heat. Stir gently, until it's almost too hot to sip (8 to 10 minutes). Don't try to speed things up by using higher heat, because the spices need time to flavor the milk. Strain the liquid into serving mugs. Garnish with the star anise.

Loco Cocoa

3 to 4 servings

ingredients

½ cup sugar
⅓ cup cocoa powder
a pinch of salt
2 teaspoons vanilla extract
4 cups milk
marshmallows (optional)

You'll need a medium-sized cooking pot. Whisk the first four ingredients in the pot with a splash of milk until it looks like fudge sauce. Gradually add the rest of the milk, stirring as you go. Make sure you don't miss any chocolate on the bottom.

Heat the pot on a stovetop over medium-high heat, stirring gently, until it's almost too hot to drink (3 to 5 minutes). If you use marshmallows, put them in the bottom of the serving mugs and ladle Loco Cocoa over them. Turn off the stove, or the cocoa will overcook.

Hot Vanilla

3 to 4 servings

ingredients

Seeds from half of a vanilla bean
   (See page 14.)
⅓ cup sugar
4 cups milk
   (Rice milk is really good in this.)

Stir the vanilla seeds and sugar together in a medium-sized cooking pot. Mash and stir until the seeds are evenly distributed except for that last clump that just won't mix in. (There's always one stubborn clump.)

Add the milk and heat on a stovetop over a medium-high burner. Stir gently, until it's almost too hot to sip (3 to 5 minutes). Turn off the stove and use a ladle to dole out servings of this delicious drink.

The Bee's Knees

Sour, sweet, and steamy...mmm! Hot honey lemonade will warm you right up. Enjoy it any time you want, but it's especially good if you have a cold. It will soothe your sore throat and help you forget how miserable you feel.

2 to 3 servings

ingredients

¾ cup honey
½ cup fresh lemon juice (use about three lemons)
   (See page 102 for tips on juicing.)
1 ½ cups water

Combine ingredients in a small cooking pot and heat them on a stovetop over medium heat until the mixture starts to steam. Turn off the stove and use a ladle to serve the tea. Don't burn your tongue—you won't be able to taste the drink! Instead, test the temperature with a pinky.

Surprise Twists

That's what I call the garnish I like in my mug of The Bee's Knees. Use a bar zester. Pull the large hole on the side of the zester across a citrus fruit (we used lemon here) to get a long strip of zest. See photo above. Twist the strip of zest to make it curl. See photo below.

hot stuff

Mexican Hot Chocolate

This isn't the original Mexican chocolate drink. That one was served cold, used water instead of milk, and had no sugar at all. This recipe is hot, creamy, sweet, and spicy. Enjoy!

3 to 4 servings

ingredients

1 ½ ounces unsweetened baking chocolate

2 tablespoons water

4 cups milk

½ cup sugar

1 teaspoon ground cinnamon

⅛ teaspoon ground cayenne pepper (optional)

1 tablespoon vanilla extract

4 cinnamon sticks for garnish (optional)

Heat the chocolate and water in a medium-sized cooking pot over low heat. As the chocolate begins to melt, stir it constantly with a wooden spoon. When it's completely melted, **whisk** in the milk, sugar, ground cinnamon, and cayenne.

Turn the heat up to medium, and then whisk constantly until the mixture is hot and steamy. Add the vanilla extract. Turn off the heat.

For more froth, use a whisk, immersion blender or **electric frother.** Use a ladle to serve the hot chocolate. If you like, garnish each drink with cinnamon sticks and chocolate curls. See instructions at right.

Chocolate Curls
Make chocolate curls by pulling a vegetable peeler across a regular chocolate bar. Let the curls fall onto your drink.

Sensational Cinnamon Tea

The spicy sweetness of this simple, delicious tea spreads through your body, making you feel warm and happy. It might also help settle your stomach if you're feeling queasy. You can reuse the same cinnamon stick several times before it loses its flavor.

1 serving

ingredients

1 cinnamon stick
1 ½ cups water
1 teaspoon sugar

Place the cinnamon stick and water in a medium-sized pot and bring to a simmer on a stovetop over medium heat. **Simmer** for 5 to 7 minutes. Don't try to speed things up by using a higher heat setting—the cinnamon needs time to **steep.**

After simmering, fish out the cinnamon stick. (Let it dry so you can use it again sometime.) Stir the sugar into the tea. Wait for it to cool down to a sipable temperature before you taste it.

How Sweet It Is

You can make your own custom-flavored sugars to stir into hot drinks. It's easy, and you can use one of these sugars anytime a drink recipe calls for sugar.

Very Vanilla

Put a whole vanilla bean or the scraped pod in a sealed container of sugar (as much as you want). After a couple of days, you'll have vanilla sugar! You can add plain sugar to the container as it runs out—the vanilla bean will continue to flavor it for a long time.

Simple Cinnamon

Mix 1 tablespoon of ground cinnamon into ½ cup of sugar. Store in a sealed container.

Luscious Lemon

Mix 1 tablespoon finely grated lemon zest into ½ cup of sugar. Store in a sealed container.

party drinks

Get your friends together and make them one of these party drink recipes.

Neon Slurp

This punch combines exotic fruit with bright blue sports drink, plus limeade for zing and ginger ale for fizz.

about 15 servings

ingredients

1 liter blue sports drink
4 cups guava nectar
½ cup frozen limeade concentrate
1 liter ginger ale
drops of blue food coloring

Combine the sports drink, guava nectar, and frozen limeade concentrate in a punch bowl or pitcher. Just before serving, add the ginger ale. Make this punch's color even brighter by adding the food coloring.

Oh Buoy! Garnish your punches by floating slices of fruit on the surface. I used star fruit and oranges here.

89

Guanabana Cabana

Anna and Hannah were hanging out with their pet iguana. "Man, it's hot as a sauna!" complained Anna. "Have a swim," said Hannah. "Don't wanna," said Anna. "Why not?" asked Hannah. "Piranha!" shrieked Anna. So instead they cooled off with Guanabana Cabana.

about 15 servings

ingredients

one 15-ounce can of pears halves, not drained
three 11-ounce cans of guanabana nectar (about 4 cups)
1 tablespoon grenadine (a flavoring sold in the soft drink aisle of a grocery)
½ teaspoon vanilla extract
1½ liters ginger ale (about 6 cups)

Blend the pears with their juice until they are the consistency of baby food. (That's smooth.) Use a spoon to combine the pear mush with the guanabana nectar, grenadine, and vanilla extract in a large punch bowl. Just before serving, add the ginger ale. You can serve the punch over ice, since it tastes best cold.

Guanabana (also known as soursop) has a sweet, sour, vanilla taste. It is green and spiny and grows on trees in tropical regions.

Double Duty Pink and Fruity

This fantastic recipe works two ways—you can sip a Hot Magenta for a tangy, spicy treat on a cold day, or you can chill it and add soda to make a zippy party Punch Out.

Hot Magenta
3 to 4 servings

ingredients

2 oranges
4 cups pineapple juice
¼ cup cinnamon candies

Wash the oranges and cut them into ½-inch slices. (Normally you wouldn't wash oranges, because you take the peel off, but in this recipe the peel stays on and goes in your drinks.)

Combine the sliced oranges, pineapple juice, and cinnamon candies in a medium-sized cooking pot. Heat on a stovetop over a medium-hot burner.

Stir occasionally, until the candies have dissolved and the Hot Magenta is steaming. Ladle out each serving directly from the pot.

Punch Out
7 to 8 servings

ingredients

1 recipe Hot Magenta, chilled
   (See recipe on this page.)
1 liter ginger ale

Combine both ingredients in a punch bowl or pitcher with ice. Serve and enjoy.

93

party drinks

Strawberry Sweetheart

This creamy, frothy punch is like a giant ice cream float. I'm going to make it for my friend Rachel's birthday, because she loves hearts. It's also the perfect thing to serve at a Valentine's Day party. If the fresh strawberries at the grocery store don't look so great, substitute a 16-ounce package of frozen strawberries.

12 to 15 servings

ingredients

1 pint strawberries,
   washed and hulled
2 cups pineapple juice
2 tablespoons frozen orange
   juice concentrate
1 liter ginger ale
1 pint vanilla ice cream

Blend the strawberries, pineapple juice, and frozen orange juice concentrate until smooth. Transfer the mixture to a punch bowl. Just before serving, add the ginger ale and plop the ice cream right in the middle.

The Opposite Of A Ring Of Fire

Keeping punch cold can be a challenge—small ice cubes tend to melt, diluting the flavor of the punch. One solution is to make an ice ring like this one. Just freeze water in a bundt pan. (I used a heart-shaped one here, and added whole strawberries for decoration.) Run hot water over the bottom of the pan to help release the ice ring.

Knock-Your-Socks-Off
Key Lime Punch

This is a version of the punch my stepmother, Beverly, made for my wedding. It's zingy and refreshing; perfect to serve at a cookout.

12 to 15 servings

ingredients

12-ounce bottle of key lime juice
double recipe of Knock Your Socks Off Ginger Ale
   syrup (recipe on page 51)
2 liters sparkling water (seltzer or club soda)
a dash of bitters (found with cocktail mixers at the grocery store)
2 drops of green food coloring (optional)
lime slices for garnish

Stir everything but the sparkling water together in a punch bowl. Wait until the beginning of the party to add ice and sparkling water or you'll have flat, watery punch. (You don't want that.) Serve by ladling into cups.

If you can't find key lime juice from Florida, squeeze enough lime halves to get 1 1/2 cups of fresh juice. (About 6 whole limes.)

Razzle Dazzle

Dazzle your friends with this sparkling raspberry lemonade. It's everything you could want in a punch—fruity, sour-sweet, and fizzy. And it turns your tongue red if you drink a lot. It's guaranteed to be a hit at your party.

10 to 12 servings

ingredients

juice of six lemons (about 1 cup)
12-ounce package of frozen raspberries, thawed
1½ cups sugar
2 liters sparkling water (seltzer water or club soda)

Get the pulp of the raspberries (see instructions on right) and put it in a medium-sized cooking pot. Add the lemon juice and sugar to the pot. Heat on a stovetop over medium heat, stirring constantly, until the sugar has dissolved and the mixture looks glossy. This takes about 5 minutes.

Let the raspberry mixture cool. (Don't forget to turn off the stove!) Just before serving, combine the raspberry mixture and sparkling water in a punch bowl. Ladle each serving into a cup of ice. After a few sips, stick out your tongue and have a friend tell you if it's turned colors yet.

Getting Raspberry Pulp

Use a rubber spatula to mash the raspberry pulp through the strainer and into the pot. You might want to do this in two batches.

98

party drinks

Swait Tay

Southerners don't make "sweet tea," we make "swait tay." "Swait" sounds like pure Southern dialect to me, but I recently learned that when British people colonized America, all English-speakers said, "tay," for "tea." My guess is that the pronunciation stayed the same in the South all these years. However you choose to say it, this is a refreshing drink.

6 to 8 servings

ingredients

2 lemons

2 jumbo-size black teabags (the tea's black, not the bags)

1 cup sugar

1 quart water, boiling

1 quart cold water

ice

lemon slices for garnish (optional)

Squeezing a Teabag

This is a cool tip. To get all the flavor and liquid out of a teabag without burning your fingers or making a big mess, just squeeze the teabag between two spoons.

Cut the lemons in half and put them in a pitcher with the teabags and sugar. Pour the boiling water in on top of them. Let the tea steep for 5 minutes, and then fish out the teabags, squeeze them out, and discard them. Add the cold water to the pitcher. Serve the drink over ice with a slice of lemon. Practice your Southern accent while enjoying your Swait Tay.

First Ades

These refreshing recipes make plenty to share. For a zingy variation, add a chunk of peeled fresh ginger to the sugar water and let it simmer for five minutes after the sugar has dissolved.

Use these instructions for all three recipes:

Grab a cutting board and roll the fruits between your hand and the cutting board. This softens the fruits so you can get more juice from each. Then use a knife to cut the fruits in half and squeeze out the juice. Pour the juice through a strainer to remove the seeds.

Combine the sugar and water in a medium-sized cooking pot and heat it on a stovetop over medium heat. Stir occasionally, until the sugar has dissolved (about 2 minutes).

Put the ice in a large plastic pitcher or punch bowl—don't use a glass container, because it might crack from the temperature change. Pour the sugar-water and fruit juice over the ice. Stir until the ice melts. Serve over ice. Enjoy.

5 to 7 servings

Lime Time

12 limes (about 2 cups of juice)

2 cups sugar

4 cups water

6 cups ice

4 to 6 servings

Pucker Up

8 lemons (about 1½ cups of juice)

2 cups sugar

4 cups water

5 cups ice

5 to 7 servings

Ultimate Orange

15 oranges (about 5 cups of juice)

1 lemon (almost ¼ cup of juice)

½ cup sugar

1 cup water

2 cups ice

Ring Around The Rim

Make a sour drink fancy—and give it some sweetness—by sugaring the rim of the glass. Run a wedge of lemon or lime around the rim to wet it. Then put a couple of tablespoons of sugar in a small, shallow dish such as a saucer. Roll the wetted rim of the glass through the sugar to coat it.

Agua de Tamarindo

Tamarinds are popular fruits in Africa, India, and Central America. I can buy them at the regular ol' grocery store in my town, but depending on where you live, you may have to go to a market that specializes in items from Latin America or Asia. If they don't carry the fresh pods like you see here, they will probably have frozen pulp. Use 2 ounces.

3 to 5 servings

ingredients

1/2 pound tamarinds (8 tamarinds should do the trick)
3/4 to 1 cup sugar
6 cups water, boiling

Shell the tamarinds. (See instructions on right.) Put the tamarind pulp and 3/4 cup of sugar in a heat-proof mixing bowl and pour the boiling water over it. Let the mixture soak for at least two hours or overnight. (Put it in the refrigerator if you leave it overnight.)

Use your clean hands and/or the back of a wooden spoon to mush the pulp away from the seeds. If this isn't super-easy, let the mixture soak longer. I'm sorry I can't be more specific about soaking times—it depends on how fresh the tamarinds are! Discard the seeds.

Ladle the mixture through a strainer into a pitcher. Use the back of a wooden spoon to mash as much juice as possible out of the pulp. Instead of throwing the pulp away, see if anyone in your family wants to experiment with it to make a sauce for meat, fish, or vegetables.

Stir the Agua de Tamarindo and have a taste. Add more sugar if it's too sour, or plain water if it's too strong. Serve over ice.

Shelling Tamarinds

Crack the outer brown pods with your hands and pull out the sticky reddish pulp. It looks like something from a science-fiction movie! Remove the stringy fibers that run along the sides. Just use the pulp in this recipe.

Which Cider You On?

My two favorite things about autumn are kicking through crackly fallen leaves when I take a walk and sipping hot apple cider when I get home. If you live in an area with apple orchards, you can find freshly pressed apple cider for sale in the fall.

3 to 4 servings

ingredients

4 cups apple cider
3-inch strip of lemon zest
1 cinnamon stick
6 whole cloves
⅛ teaspoon ground nutmeg
¼ teaspoon vanilla extract
extra cinnamon sticks for garnish (optional)

Combine all ingredients in a medium-sized cooking pot and simmer over a medium-hot burner for at least 5 minutes. (The longer it simmers, the spicier it tastes.) Ladle each serving directly from the pot. Turn off the stove.

You drank the whole batch but still want more? Okay. Just add as much cider as you like to the spices in the pot and simmmer again.

Mull It Over

This drink is just right for winter holidays, especially if you have a piece of gingerbread to munch on the side. I made this recipe really big so you can share it with grandparents, cousins, and friends who are visiting. For a smaller crowd, divide the recipe in half (half of 3 quarts is 6 cups). Or make the full recipe and store any leftovers in a sealed container in the refrigerator.

12 servings

ingredients

2 oranges
24 whole cloves
3 quarts cranberry juice cocktail
1 cup honey
2 cinnamon sticks
2 whole star anise
piece of fresh ginger the size of your thumb,
  peeled and sliced into ¼-inch rounds

Studding an Orange
Cut an orange into quarters. Stick three cloves into the rind of each orange piece.

Stud the oranges with the cloves (see instructions on this page), and then combine all of the ingredients in a medium-sized cooking pot. Heat the pot on a stovetop over a medium-hot heat, stirring occasionally. Let the mixture simmer for at least 5 minutes. Ladle the drink into mugs to serve. If you're not drinking it all at once, just turn the burner down to low to hold Mull It Over at the right serving temperature.

Turn off the burner when the pot's empty or you'll have a burnt, sticky mess to clean up!

Glossary

almond milk. whitish, yummy, nutritious liquid made from almonds and water

bacteria. microscopic, single-celled organisms that are basically everywhere. Most bacteria are harmless or helpful, but some types can make you sick, so wash all fruits and veggies before you eat them.

bar zester. a kitchen tool for making fancy garnishes from the zest of citrus fruits

blade. the sharp part of a knife, blender, or food processor, which does the cutting

blend. to use a blender to purée ingredients until drinkable

blender. See Immersion Blender and Standing Blender

boil. what happens to a liquid when it gets hot enough to evaporate—there are lots of big bubbles

bruises. soft, brown places where a piece of produce has been injured

bulb. the widest part of an immersion blender

chilled. refrigerated until cool

citrus fruit. fruits with thick peels and sections of pulp, such as oranges, lemons, and limes

colander. a piece of kitchen equipment that looks like a bowl with holes in it, which is used to rinse or drain foods

combine. to mix ingredients together until they're evenly distributed

core. the tough, not-delicious part in the very middle of some fruits, such as pineapples and apples

cored. describes fruit after the core has been removed

cows' milk. white, delicious, calcium-rich liquid squeezed from cows' udders. I recommend drinking the organic kind. See Organic.

cube. a six-sided solid with all sides equal. (Don't worry about cutting food for these recipes into perfect cubes. Just cut it into chunks that are close to cubes.)

cutting board. a kitchen tool that protects your countertop from being cut by a knife

dilute. to make the flavor of a drink weaker, usually with water. It's good to dilute the lemon juice in Pucker Up lemonade (you don't want too much pucker!), but not so great to dilute punch with melted ice.

electric frother. a neat electrical kitchen tool that you dip into drinks to make them foamy and thick

farmers' markets. places where farmers get together to sell what they grow. You can usually find the freshest produce at farmers' markets.

ginger root. a gnarly, pale tan root with a spicy, zingy flavor, which you can find in the produce section of the grocery store

grater. a kitchen tool with small, sharp holes that you rub food against to get smaller pieces of the food

grating. using a grater to cut a piece of food into smaller pieces. See Grater.

growth hormones. medicines given to cows to make them grow faster so they will make food faster, which are then found in the cow's milk

halving. cutting something into two equal pieces

hulled. the stem and leaves have been removed

immersion blender. a handheld electrical appliance used to blend or purée foods to make them drinkable

in season. describes produce that is naturally ripe at a certain time of year

knife. a kitchen tool for cutting

lengthwise. along the longest side

liquefied. turned into liquid. You know what liquid is, right?

liquid measuring cups. kitchen tools for getting the right amounts of liquid ingredients, such as milk, when you pour up to the line you want

measuring cups. kitchen tools for getting the perfect amounts of dry or solid ingredients

measuring spoons. kitchen tools for getting small amounts of ingredients

organic. this generally refers to food grown and produced without chemical fertilizers, pesticides, additives, or artificial colorings or flavorings. Governments and certification boards have different standards of what organic means, but any kind of organic food is probably better for you and the environment than non-organic food.

pesticides. things sprayed on plants so that bugs (pests) won't eat them before you can. Chemical pesticides can be bad for you, so wash all fruits and veggies before you eat them

pit. the large seed in the middle of fruits like mangos, avocados, and peaches

pod. the outer covering that holds the seeds of some plants

produce. fruits and vegetables

purée. to use a blender to liquefy ingredients

rice milk. white, yummy, protein-rich liquid made from rice and water

rind. the thick peel of melons

ripe. fully grown and ready to be eaten

ripen. to become ripe

ripeness. the state of being fully grown and ready to be eaten

seeds. the part of fruit that can grow a new plant

shelling. removing the outer pod from seeds

soymilk. white, tasty, nutritious liquid made from soybeans and water

spines. poky, pointy things that are very unpleasant to eat

standing blender. an electrical appliance that sits on the countertop, used to blend or purée ingredients to make them drinkable. Don't forget to put the lid on!

steep. to allow hot liquids to pull flavor out of tea or spices

stem scar. the rougher round place where a piece of fruit was attached to the stem of the plant it grew on. There is a smaller blossom scar on the other end where the flower fell off.

stir. to use a spoon to combine ingredients

submerged. underneath liquid

thunk test. testing a watermelon's ripeness using the move where you hold the tip of your middle finger behind your thumb and then release it forcefully against your brother's head and say, "What? I didn't do anything!" A ripe watermelon sounds hollow when you thunk it.

unripe. not yet fully grown and ready to be eaten

vanilla beans. the flavorful fruit of the vanilla orchid, which can be found at gourmet or health-food stores (if your grocery doesn't sell them)

vegetable peeler. a kitchen tool used to remove the peel of thin-skinned fruits and veggies

wedges. the crescent shapes that you cut round foods such as honeydew into before you peel and chop them

whisk. a kitchen tool made of curved or coiled wires that's used to whip or froth ingredients

yield. the number of servings that a recipe makes

zest. the outermost, colored part of the peel of citrus fruits

Index

acknowledgments, 112
almond milk, 11, making, 47
apple, cider, 106, juice, 29, 40, 44, 46
apricot nectar, 17, 21
avocado, 11, 30
banana, 12, 17, 18, 21, 25, 29, 34, 58, 66
bee balm, 55
berries, mixed, 24
black cherry soda, 65
black tea, 101
blending, terms and techniques, 15
blueberries, 5, 24, 57
brown sugar, 81
cantaloupe, 21, 33, 52
caramel, 26, 70, candies, 70
cayenne pepper, 85
celery salt, 22
chamomile, 55
chocolate, ice cream, 58, 61, 65, recipes using, 85, sandwich cookies, 61, syrup, 34, unsweetened baking, 85. *See also* Cocoa Powder
cinnamon, 29, 47, 74, 85, candies, 93, stick, 52, 81, 85, 87, 106,
cloves, 81, 106, 109
club soda. *See* sparkling water
cocoa powder, 66, 81
coconut cream, sweetened, 43, 77
coconut milk, unsweetened, 34, 74
cooking, terms and techniques, 15
cranberry juice cocktail, 109
cucumber, 22, 43
cutting terms and techniques, 12
freezing fruits, 14
fruit pancake syrup, 66
gelatin, 40

ginger, 33, 51, 110, how to peel, 13
ginger ale, 40, 48, 51, 89, 90, 93, 94
glossary, 110
grape juice concentrate, 39
grenadine, 48, 90
guanabana, 90, juice, 36, nectar, 90
guava nectar, 89
hibiscus, 55
honey, 17, 30, 33, 47, 82, 109
honeydew melon, 13, 37
ice, 22, 43, 48, 74, 102, ring, how to make an, 94
ice cream, 57, 61, 62, 66, 69, 70, 73, 78
key lime juice, 97
kiwi, 37
knives, using, 12
lemon, 22, 44, 82, 98, 101, 102, 106
lemon balm, 55
lime, 74, 78, 102
limeade concentrate, 43, 89
mango, 42, 74
maraschino cherries, 48, 65
marshmallows, 81
measuring, 14
metric conversions, 112
milk, 11, 30, 34, 57, 58, 61, 66, 69, 70, 78, 81, 85, sweetened condensed, 74
mint leaves, 43, 55
mixing, 14
nutmeg, 17, 43, 47, 106
nuts, recipes using, 18, 28, 47, 61, 66
oats, 18
orange, 93, 102, 109, juice, 18, 26, 73, juice concentrate, 32, 73, 94
papaya, 21

peach, 17, 21, 47, nectar, 33
peanut butter, 18, 28, 66
peanut butter cups, 61
pear, canned halves, 90, nectar, 33, 34
pepper, bell 22
peppermint, candies, 69, extract, 69
pineapple, 34, 70, 77, juice, 17, 21, 30, 77, 93, 94
pomegranate juice, 21
raspberries, 58, 98, how to get pulp, 98
rice, 52
rice milk, 11, 30, 52, 81
root beer, 62
salt, 32, 81
sassafras, 51, 55
seltzer water. See sparkling water
serving tips, 15
sherbet, 62
shopping, 11
soda, 62, 65

soymilk, 11, 34
sparkling water, 39, 44, 51, 98
sports drink, 89
star anise, 81, 109
star fruit, 89
strawberries, 17, 18, 24, 34, 74, 94, how to hull, 14
sugar, 22, 43, 51, 52, 85, 101, 102, 105
sugaring rims, 102
sweet potato, 26
tamarinds, 105
tomato, 22
vanilla, extract, 81, 85, 90, 106, ice cream, 57, 61, 66, 69, 70, 73, 78, soda, 62
vanilla bean, 14, 51, 87
watermelon, 13, 33
whipped cream, 65
yam, 26
yogurt, 11, 17, 26, 43
zest, 40, 78, 82

Acknowledgments

Thanks to everyone who worked so hard to make this book. Special thanks to our models, Erin, Eva, Gus, Katie, Jasmine, Liz, Mali, Michael, and Twana; Stylist extraordinaire Skip Wade; Copy Editor Judy Berndt; and the milkshake-tasting team, Steve, Eva, Andrew, and Courtney.

Metric Conversions

To convert degrees Fahrenheit to degrees Celsius, subtract 32 and then multiply by .56.
To convert inches to centimeters, multiply by 2.5.
To convert ounces to grams, multiply by 28.
To convert teaspoons to milliliters, multiply by 5.
To convert tablespoons to milliliters, multiply by 15.
To convert fluid ounces to milliliters, multiply by 30.
To convert cups to liters, multiply by .24.